is an internationally-acclaimed independent publishing house, literary journal, and arts organisation dedicated to the celebration of music in all of its forms. Half Mystic Press, our publishing arm, releases two to three books of prose, poetry, and experimental work per year—invocations of love, wildness, and uncertainty, the heartbeat of humanity set to a 4/4 time signature, expanding and redefining unsung narratives, sharp and lamenting, eyes on the horizon. For more information, books similar to this one, and submission guidelines, please visit www.halfmystic.com.

Praise for Waiting for Frank Ocean in Cairo

"*Waiting for Frank Ocean in Cairo* is an exceptional example of a writer blending life and the world life moves through so seamlessly that the two become one. These poems are tender, vivid, and touchable. Hazem Fahmy is a writer of immense care, and immense patience, and that care appears not only on a line level, but in an even greater way: in the opening of a palm and the whispering of *I'd like to show you something that means the world to me.*"

—Hanif Abdurraqib, author of *They Can't Kill Us Until They Kill Us* and *Go Ahead in the Rain: Notes to A Tribe Called Quest*

"Hazem Fahmy's sophomore collection is a feast. Purposeful, international, intersectional, and lyrical, the poems are heartbreakingly attuned to the conversations of Fahmy's generation. Frank Ocean is a light post, a guiding vision of how one narrates the highway of a budding and beautiful life 'split over oceans,' and a long and slow road trip soundtrack. Devour these poems. Enjoy the innocence and decadence of *Waiting*'s magical ride."

> —Shayla Lawson, author of *This Is Major: Notes on Diana Ross, Dark Girls & Being Dope* and *I Think I'm Ready to See Frank Ocean*

"Hazem Fahmy is a poet of preservation. If a museum is a house that cares for, and displays, objects and vignettes of the past, then *Waiting for Frank Ocean in Cairo* is a museum. In it is a keen and compelling exhibition of haunting artifacts and moments from the speaker's childhood in Egypt: evidence of a resistance to erasure and forgetting, even through migration to America. 'I am still learning to forget the house / I learned to cook in. The house I stopped speaking / of love in,' Fahmy writes. Part family album, part map across the geographies that have shaped his life—from Cairo's many highways to L.A., Houston, and the Hudson—this book asserts the voice of a poet concerned at once with the minutely domestic and the transnational. In refreshingly honest, unadorned lyric, the poems on display here bring us into the world of a boy who wants nothing more than to dance to the backdrop of wreckage and newness, in a city 'in love with its fences.'"

> —Sara Elkamel, author of *Field of No Justice*

FIRST PRINTING, MARCH 2022
HALF MYSTIC PRESS
www.halfmystic.com

COPYRIGHT © HAZEM FAHMY, 2022

EDITED *by* DANIE SHOKOOHI
and COURTNEY FELLE

COVER ART *by* MAURI VALENTINE
DESIGNED *by* TOPAZ WINTERS

ALL RIGHTS RESERVED

You know the drill: except for quotation of short passages for the purpose of critical review, no part of this publication may be reproduced in any form or by any means, electronic or print, including photocopying, recording, or by any information storage and retrieval system, without the prior permission in writing from the author and Half Mystic Press.

Don't steal art. Authors need to eat too.

ISBN-13: 978-1-948552-11-0
ISBN-10: 1-948552-11-6

Waiting for Frank Ocean in Cairo

Hazem Fahmy

A Half Mystic Press Publication

For سی, who believed in this project when I didn't

Table of Contents

In Which I Pause Frank, but Still Do Not Speak	1
Don't Die	4
All Summer I Waited for Frank	6
On the Highway, to the Tune of "Solo (Reprise)"	9
Interrogation of the New Year, to the Tune of "Novacane"	11
On the Highway, to the Tune of "Nights"	12
Interrogation of Male Tears, to the Tune of "Bad Religion"	14
Frank Haunts Me Across a Decade	16
Night Anthem	19
Faith Is the Substance	21

Still Life of Reunion,
to the Tune of "Thinkin Bout You"   23

Still Life of Teita's Balcony,
to the Tune of "Futura Free"   26

In Which I Prefer to Blast Frank
With Door Closed   28

Still Life of Reunion,
to the Tune of "Close to You"   31

U-N-I-T-Y   34

Interrogating My Family's Living Room(s),
to the Tune of "Skyline To"   36

Family Interrogation,
to the Tune of "Pink + White"   39

Portrait of My Father as the Laundry Machine   41

It's All Downhill From Here   43

Interrogating How We Forget Our Father(s),
to the Tune of "Forrest Gump"   45

Acknowledgements 48

About the Author 49

In Which I Pause Frank, but Still Do Not Speak

Once again my father makes
his way into the house and I do not
rise to meet him. I sit

>   in the warm spot on
>   the couch, watching
>   him stumble with his

few words, trying to walk
without walking all over us.
Mama stays silent,

>   smiling. Sometimes I wish I could
>   have that demeanor, but I know
>   too well what it costs. She speaks

the price. I am too young
to yell that loudly.

*I don't like to fight 'til I'm
fighting.*

Mama says I was born quiet,
barely crying. That must mean
the rage only came later (was not instinct).

> In this house, we speak silent
> language so loud, it couldn't
> fit in such small, still bodies.

High blood pressure runs on both
sides, a technical
way to say that we were born

> with this vocabulary:
> fiery nostrils, wide eyes,
> shaking fists. My father never

raised his, and I guess
I am grateful for that. Sometimes
we joke about that time

> when I was eight and found a
> handgun, Gedo's, in Teita's
> old room. I remember how

Mama kept asking me why
I hid it and I had
no answer—wasn't thinking.

    I should have said:

I was trying to keep it
    safe.

Don't Die

I should say and you should hear I've loved
I took a seat on the ice-cold lawn,

I took a walk with the palm trees as the daylight fell
every moment was so precious then

I'm Richard Gere in a tux
roaming around like I'm ready for a funeral

I'm about to drive in the ocean
the entire earth is fighting, all the world is at its end

spaceships are lifting off of a dying world
there will be tears

that's American law
there wasn't room for you and I, only you, goodbye, goodbye

land of the free
we are all mortals, aren't we? Any moment this could go

numb, numb, numb, numb
zero emotion, muted emotion, pitch corrected,

computed emotion, I've no doubt
this is the home of the brave

and millions are left behind while the sky burns
they don't mean too much

cry, cry, cry, even though that won't change a thing
I can't feel a thing,

I can't be there with you
talking to myself

All Summer I Waited for Frank

Speeding across Brooklyn on a hot July afternoon in Hanane's car, Yasmin tells me about Harper Lee. She had been reclusive, almost never in the press. An *Atlantic* article was just published, comparing the novelist to who but Frank Ocean, citing the time between projects. A fascinating similarity. Later, my feet in the sand, Adam shows me the memes:

#WaitingForFrank
#WheresTheAlbumFrank

We laugh as we get high on the beach, making do with what's been given to us.

༄

On a hotter July night, I wait for the subway with George and Julian and we discuss the act of disappearing.

Impatience wears our backs. What are we asking Frank to prove? Has the album become another form of paper(s)?

꩜

I think I waited so long for Frank because I came out of Ramadan with tired ears. Then again, Frank was instinct. As was waiting. What else was there to do as summer folded itself shut?

꩜

Before he leaves the city, Marcelo throws a going away party. In the Facebook event, he promises there will be people on shifts, waiting for the album to drop. This is August, so he feels lucky. I never make it to Yonkers. I don't know if this actually happens. I spend that night with Misho, planning what little time we have in Cairo. *This is joy, this is summer.* In the cab, I unzip my bag again, in case I forgot my passport.

#WheresTheAlbumFrank

꩜

I wake up on a Thursday in Cairo and by the grace of God the album is just there on my phone. Mama tells me to pack because we're leaving soon (second flight in seven days), but I stay in bed, headphones in. I want to dance.

My father comes in to remind me that we have to leave, so I pause the album for later. It will take me until then to realize there aren't even that many songs I can dance to.

On the Highway, to the Tune of "Solo (Reprise)"

In a grey Nissan cruising along a dark road in New Cairo,
off التسعين, Amr tells me, you have no reason to be afraid
of driving, and I think about the sweat I'm staining
into his passenger seat. I know he'd be fine
if I ask permission to smoke a cigarette, but
it's too cold outside and I don't want to roll down
the window. He says: you can't live here without a car.
I say: Gedo is 70 and hasn't touched a wheel in over 40
years. *I feel for you.* But let me tell you a story:
I have this friend who once hit and killed a man who was
trying to cross طريق المطار in the dark. This was two years
ago, but she still can't drive, says she is too traumatized.
But how can you blame her?
Knowing you have the power to take a life like that. Still,
Amr asks: why was this man running along so late in the
night, on such a dark road. I mean, it's not his fault,
البقاء لله, I don't want to desecrate a memory, let the dead
rest. But still, it's not her fault either, you know?

So low no more high horses. We rush past the uncoordinated mini mansions still being built. The few finished ones have erect streetlights and every other pole droops, unlit. I forget if the car was actually a Nissan or a Subaru, but I remember fumbling through the side roads until we saw other headlights cutting through the darkness. I remember following them until we found the right exit into الرحاب and back to my house.

Interrogation of the New Year, to the Tune of "Novacane"

6 A.M. on the first day of the year *(I can't feel my face)*
and the mosque behind the high-rise
bellows, almost at us.

أستغفر الله

We're out of hash *(I got what I wanted)* so
we laugh our way around
the balcony. This Joe guy
asks me about the future,
asks what I intend to do
in America, asks if I plan
on bringing my cousin with me.

I don't use my words, my snort
does fine. He asks
if I am Muslim, and I want to ask
if he really wants to know
the answer.

On the Highway, to the Tune of "Nights"

I don't want [a] conversation so I convince Misho to play Frank as we swerve off المحور and unto Nasr City, "Nights" blasting from Agha's car speakers, Laila bouncing beside me. The patches of shanty shacks disappear as the high-rise lights approach. We hit a pothole, and I almost bump my head, but Frank keeps me unfazed. I smile manically, *breathe 'til I evaporate*, as I sing along, and this is a performance of sorts. Everyone knows I am American, and Americanized. The second is perhaps more important. But they don't know what kind of American I am, so I need to show them. I learned a long time ago that anyone with a blue passport is apple pie here. *I don't trust them anyways.* But I taste differently, والله. I am apple pie and بسبوسة and some days that is too decadent for a single mouth so I laugh loudly, sugary saliva drips down my lips, unto the night air where it can find somewhere better to make a cavity out of a lone boy.

Interrogation of Male Tears, to the Tune of "Bad Religion"

I can never make [men] *love me.*

I have heard this stifled song
before: my father whimpers
in the living room while I hide
behind the couch. In a cab

racing from Maadi
to rehab, Misho cries
for the first time in what feels
like years, and the sight stops me.

The climax of a movie
I've been waiting to see, but
could never name. I only heard
the story, of how Amir

wept endlessly over the phone
to Mama while driving

on some Boston highway, but
I can imagine how it

sounded like screeching to her.
I hear how sweet the static
must have sounded when
the connection cut off.

Frank Haunts Me Across a Decade

Every other day a phone call from across the world
brings me to my knees, a micro-sob story I recount
in the mirror. Every time the connection cuts off, the
sound evaporates like a stolen breath. Frank, the specter
of all my summers—the unmentionable shadow—dyed
his hair green and suddenly there was an entire field
of possibilities, reminiscent of the constellation of clubs
off the highway in Houston. From the airport, all worlds
seem possible, ones lost and forgotten. I was never one
for making a saint out of anything, let alone a man
who makes music I cry to. On a rare cold morning
in Austin, I biked to a theater, unsettlingly aware
of my own temporal nature. In L.A.,
Frank was the soundtrack to every car ride, even
though I never played him once. In Houston,
Frank haunted the stereo, became the call
of the American night. I despise how wide
the world seemed, the sheer unfathomability

of a highway ending, let alone an ocean
running out of water. I have known nights
of ungodly solitude. Yet I have also known
the catastrophe of the unexpected phone call,
that everyday shit. The concert was not the holy
site I once led myself to believe. Music, at the end
of the day, can only do so much. I am learning to call
things disruptive instead of radical. Once, hair, sweat
and bad breath became the monikers of the night,
and it was intoxicating. My fear of the mosh pit
never left. I never wanted a single house to be
my world. I am still learning to forget the house
I learned to cook in. The house I stopped speaking
of love in. The house I learned to trust
hands other than mine in. The last couch I slept on
said something about where I was with my father then.
That time, I listened. The cold walk home could be a slow
hell, but it could also be a still kind of heaven. I no longer
await the day I will be happy. A stupid kind of progress.
I have not forgotten that house. Wordlessly I announced
my desperation. I claimed to dream
of a still mind, but I was lying. If you had asked me
what I wanted that year, I would have told you I wanted
to be loved, but even that would not have been enough.
Perhaps the more honest answer: I wanted
the fleeing ecstasy only possible in the minutes
of a Frank Ocean song. I wanted
to admit that I was *a mess in America* and be okay

with it. I wanted endless phone calls, to be harangued
ceaselessly by those who needed me. I wanted
and I wanted
and I wanted,

Night Anthem

Some nights I am seized
with an almost uncontrollable desire to banish
Frank from my library. I grow weary
of passion. Some nights I lie
awake in bed listening,
knowing I have doomed
myself to a restless sleep. In ten years,
I never hung a poster of Frank on my wall.

The nights I need unreachable men
to croon me to sleep are less frequent. More common
is the night I crave an isolation I know
I will despise. The brief walls of my closet,
lined with unread books. Every year
I face them and promise they will be no more. I calculate

how many books I would need
to read per week for that to happen. I shut
the door to my closet and lie in bed. I move
on from the almost uncontrollable desire. I am
reminded by my love that whoever convinced me

that time was precarious did not have
my best interests at heart. That includes
myself. I do not

attempt to cease the day. I attempt
to rest at night. I reject the call
of music. I delete the playlist
with the saddest Frank songs. I go
to sleep without reading.

Faith Is the Substance

I'm a mess in America
the truth is obsolete

our daughters and our sons
are candles in the sun

you don't know how little you matter
until you're all alone

underneath our legion's view
feet covered in cut flowers

some fertilizer
I found you laying with Samson and his full head of hair

we escaped him
hopped into my car, drove far

in the sky up above, the birds
domesticated paradise, palm trees and pools

life in the clouds
in the middle of Arkansas

it's happiness
I saw the sky like I never seen before

with no mask on and a rusty revolver
nothing mattered

grey matter
blue matter

I never ask for much
I'll take bullshit if that's all you got

I'm not going back home, no
I won't be going backwards

Still Life of Reunion, to the Tune of "Thinkin Bout You"

It's been five years, but the boy
still shines when he smiles. I stare
at his jaw as we shiver
on the rooftop of a run-
down hotel, waiting for the waiter
to bring his beer. He says:

a lot of kids used to hook up
here, get rooms downstairs
and just go for it. But the police
have been rolling through
lately, so it's getting tough,
like everything in this country.
We laugh,

unsure why—perhaps the weight
of being neither here nor there.

*My eyes don't shed tears, but, boy,
they bawl.*

The truth is, I say, my legs
are split over the ocean.
Later, we leave this place, into
a howling night.
We notice a police car,
or بوكس parked idly outside

the hotel. We grit our teeth,
the best we can do.
I recall the moment
white Americans around
me started learning how to
fear the police, or at least

understand why others do.
I wish I knew what that
sweet innocence tasted like.
I wish I didn't have so
many names for so many
بوكسات so I tell him: I never
needed a brown boy's
body to remind me that
no state works for us, starting
with our own.

How could I forget.

He says goodbye as I get
into a cab. I say good
bye back, choke on Arabic.
He laughs. I close the door.

The instinct would be to call
him the next day—let's do it
again sometime. Instead I wait
for the summer, don't message
in between.

Still Life of Teita's Balcony, to the Tune of "Futura Free"

Mama sits on Teita's chair
by the living room window
overlooking the burnt down
Old Cairo police building.
It is morning, and the sun
lets me see every cloud
of dust dance on the balcony.

Roots run deep.

She asks me why I am still
awake, and I say: I have assumed
the form of my own
insomnia, jet lag of diaspora, always
on the move, never in one place
for supper or summer.

I'm just a guy.

But I sometimes wish the night
was a field of budding roses,
stretching from the Nile
to the Hudson, wide enough
to get lost in, small enough
to never need to call my
[Mama] *like:* [Mama] come get

me. There are no windows
in this house.

In Which I Prefer to Blast Frank With Door Closed

In our house, I wince
every time my father opens

a door, even when he's on the way
out. He swings them, one

after another, his instinct
a war he can't win. The walls shake

and shiver. The house
a museum of rage. There,

the black mark in my brother's
room, from where Mama threw

the شبشب or there,
the sad face

I Sharpied on the balloon
Amir inflated, still gazing back

at me from the ceiling
of my bedroom. Or here, this bed.

It is morning and I hear
my father shuffle around

the living room, so I raise
the volume on "Ivy." On cue, my phone

warns me: Your hearing
is important. I remind my phone

that I hear just fine: Amir
turning over in his sleep,

Mama dropping cutlery
in the sink, my father once again

slamming a door. Our house has always
been a museum of rage. I can pick any

corner to prove it. Sometimes
I want to forget

and sometimes I want to cry
over a memory I

never asked to have. *I could
hate you now,* but I'd rather

never. Instead I raise
the volume. Drown out the rest

of the house.

Still Life of Reunion, to the Tune of "Close to You"

Midnight in a cool January, and I am
throwing up in a boy's bathroom, one I once knew
intimately, but not enough to keep in touch after
he moved to Saudi Arabia, before I moved
to South Africa. The rest is ancient
history and I recall it at the slightest
whisper.

I throw up in his bathroom and he offers water,
maybe a pill to calm your poor stomach down? But all
I can think about is Mama's paranoia. Suddenly I
imagine a scenario in which he put something in
the beers to make me puke, and now he is giving
me

this pill so that something else might happen and
I know this is a dumb fucking theory, so I open
the door, thank him, and take the (Precetol?) and it

does calm my poor stomach down, so I eventually
emerge, laughing weakly, holding my mess of a
body,

rambling about how funny it is that I had such
an intimate experience in his bathroom so soon
after seeing his face again. The next day
I get to relive it, but this time I am crying
in an Ocean Basket as Mama and my aunt wait for
me

back at the table outside this clean bathroom so
we can order some fish and have a quality
lunch with Gedo and Teita, before Mama leaves
me alone in that cold house with my father for
the next few weeks. They're waiting for me but
I

(don't have much longer)

am crying in the men's bathroom and I am
not sure why, so I blame myself for forgetting to
get more Xanax from America. Such a silly mistake,
I start to feel ashamed, but remember it has actually
nothing to do with the act of crying itself, rather the
fact

(I wasn't devastated)

that I had to get up and walk briskly to the men's
bathroom of this Ocean Basket, which is so
clean, in order to cry, and I know this wouldn't
have happened in America, I would've cried
where I was, told the waiter to fuck off if he'd dared
give

me a look, but there is always a there and a here
and I suppose sometimes I should choose
which helps me breathe easier, so when I
come out of the bathroom I text the boy again
and we meet, this time in this new burger place
everyone's been talking about, even though he's a
vegetarian.

U-N-I-T-Y

there's no place to hide out here
in the morning light

when I don't have the strength
we've been here before

sometimes it's hard to tell you
where the trees burn down

our hands are filthy
blurring, blurring the line

you may not be in the mood to learn
but at your best you are love

what could I do to know you better than I do now?
infatuation's your rush

it's your choice in the end
hit the road and get rich

hope the water's deep enough
you could put a hole in the ground

take the bully on the greenest grasses
this what I would do just to show you

what you think you know
still motion pictures shot at high frequency

signal lost, pay phone, that white light
Xenons with the blue color

shine for real
where the fields went down in flames

oh, seasons dance for rain
there are times when I find

enough time to know, know nothing at all

Interrogating My Family's Living Room(s), to the Tune of "Skyline To"

In my family, every man
    has a spot in every
        living room that is claimed with

out speaking. The same goes
    for television channels. These
        decisions stay static for

years. But every other summer
    I come back from
        America and they've changed.

    Everything grows.

The other day I asked
>   my father why he started
>   >   to watch *Russia Today*

as the newscaster said
>   something about Aleppo
>   >   being "liberated." My father

said he can't trust what
>   Americans say any
>   >   more. Years ago, Gedo used

to watch *Al-Jazeera*, but
>   that was pre-Revolution.
>   >   Last summer I walked in

on him and Teita watching a
>   pirated WWE channel
>   >   with Arabic commentary.

I wondered why he spends
>   the little free time he has
>   >   with these blond men, with their sweaty

long hair and oily over
>   sized bodies. I watch them dance
>   >   across their rings, throw metal

chairs, quick tantrums, full words. I argued
    with Teita for five
        minutes about whether or

not the fighting was real. Of
    course it is, she said. Look
        at all that blood. There's

    so much blood.

Family Interrogation, to the Tune of "Pink + White"

At the annual family reunion, two hours
before the New Year, Sawsan asks me
what exactly do I do there: at that American
college I go to. She means

to ask about the daily
basis. I do not tell her
about the beer-coated dance
floors or the cigarettes

before class. I don't mention
white people who mispronounce
my name. *That's the way every
day goes.* So I tell her that I write
(weekly) for the school newspaper,
even though I have not

sent them a piece in over
a year. She smiles, asks

if I write about home,
and I tell the truth, for once.
I would, but there's just
no demand for it: You know
how Americans love to
get what they ask for. She frowns.

Says: دي مش حجة . That's no
excuse.

Portrait of My Father as the Laundry Machine

A strange man is coming
to fix it tomorrow.

It uses too much soap and water, leaves
my clothes stiff and hoarse.

I have the privilege to call it names, complain
about my clothes when it gets them wrong.

The water's exactly what I [expected].
Everything I thought it would be.

Once Mama leaves I'll
buy the bleach.

Mama's not taking responsibility
for how me and Amir's clothes turn out

anymore. She says:

You're big boys now.
You can figure it out
for yourselves.

It's All Downhill From Here

I could hate you now
so low that I can admit

it's hell on earth and the city's on fire
no, you can't make everybody equal

that's fucked up
start over right now

in the wake of a hurricane
you kneel down to the dry land

I can't believe you
want to see nirvana, but don't want to die yet

(in the dark)
it's a free world

I didn't care to state the plain
I'll be honest, I wasn't devastated

kept my mouth closed
I know you love to talk

if I was being honest
I'm not brave

you left when I forgot to speak
and that's life

just like me
there were things you didn't need to say

we have good discussion
the start of nothing

maybe I'm a fool
living so the last night feels like a past life

acid on me like the rain
it was virtual, made no sense

after twenty years in, I'm so naïve I was under
the impression I'd do anything for you

I could dream all night
drive all night

how far is a light year?

Interrogating How We Forget Our Father(s), to the Tune of "Forrest Gump"

We forget that broad shouldered
men, with pursed smiles, love the look
of our bodies in the night.
I don't care for uniforms.
What is another man
on another chair? Give me
a couch and I will be grateful.
Give me a suit and I will
laugh the summer away. I never
needed a tight pair
of pants to tell me how
to stand. Give me a couch
and I will sit down.

My back is breaking.

                              I've been playing violent
                              video games when my father
                              is around. I don't know
                              if that's because I'm bored or
                         if it has something to do with the air
                              around him, how it leaves
                              skid marks in my nostrils,
                         ash on my tongue. I don't think
                              about it too much. Keep
                              playing. Later I'll take
                         a smoke break, bite my lips.

                              They burn from the cigarettes.

We forget what we can't give.
New Cairo is in love
with its fences. Soon
there won't be much desert
to repair. There won't be
much Nile
to swim in.

But you keep running.

Hence, we forget the pages
we ripped out. Hence, I grow tired
of smoking. Give me a new lung and I will sigh softer—

remembering you.

Acknowledgements

The poems "Don't Die," "Faith is the Substance," "U-N-I-T-Y," and "It's All Downhill From Here" are centos made up, respectively, of lyrics from the Frank Ocean mixtapes *Nostalgia* and *Ultra,* and the albums *Channel Orange, Endless,* and *Blonde.*

    I am indebted and grateful to the editors of the following journals for giving earlier versions of these poems a home. Much thanks to everyone at *Bird's Thumb, Blueshift, Cordite, Hobart, Track//Four, Wildness,* and *Wyvern.*

About the Author

Hazem Fahmy is a writer and critic from Cairo. His debut chapbook, *Red//Jild//Prayer,* won the 2017 Diode Editions Contest. A Kundiman and Watering Hole Fellow, his poetry has appeared or is forthcoming in *The Best American Poetry 2020, AAWW, The Boston Review,* and *Prairie Schooner*. His criticism has appeared or is forthcoming in *The Los Angeles Review of Books, Mubi Notebook, Reverse Shot,* and *Mizna*. His performances have been featured on Button Poetry and Write About Now. He regularly writes about remakes and other media matters on Medium @hazfahmy.

www.ingramcontent.com/pod-product-compliance
Lightning Source LLC
Chambersburg PA
CBHW030139100526
44592CB00011B/956